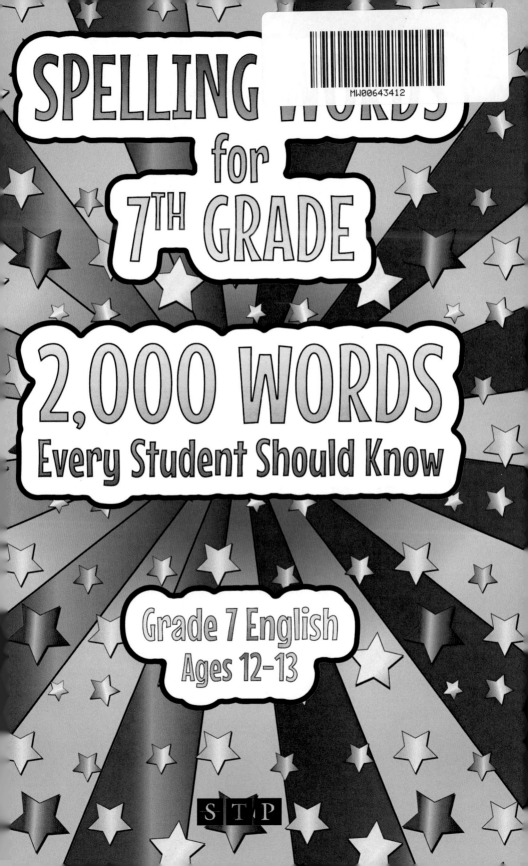

ABOUT THIS BOOK

Using a **fresh approach** to spellings lists, this illustrated collection of Spelling Words is designed **to make spelling fun** for students whilst ensuring they master essential spelling rules by the end of Grade 7.

Containing **2,000** carefully selected **level-appropriate** words, this book is made up of **70** Themed Spellings Lists that

- Have **brightly-colored illustrated backgrounds** and **engaging titles**
- Cover **loads of topics** that **actually interest students** such as social media, photography, and spies
- Relate to other **areas covered at school** including physics, World War I, and figures of speech
- Target **key words that students overuse** (e.g. 'boring', 'lucky', and 'surprised')
- Quietly introduce **specific areas of spelling** that students need to know (e.g. Greek & Latin root words, word building, and homophones & near homophones)
- Are made up of **25 to 30 words each**

HOW TO USE IT

All the **lists are self-contained**, so you can work through them **in order** or, you can dip in to use them for **focused practice**. And, as these lists are themed, they are **also a useful resource** for a range of **writing projects and exercises**.

For your convenience, an **Index** to the **spelling rules, patterns, and themed areas** dealt with by each of the lists is included at the **back of the book** on page 40.

Published by STP Books
An imprint of Swot Tots Publishing Ltd
Kemp House
152-160 City Road
London EC1V 2NX

www.swottotspublishing.com

Text, design, illustrations and layout © Swot Tots Publishing Ltd
First published 2021

Swot Tots Publishing Ltd have asserted their moral right under the Copyright, Designs and Patents Act, 1988, to be identified as the author of this work.

Typeset, cover design, and inside concept design by Swot To Publishing Ltd.

British Library Cataloguing-in-Publication Data. A catalog record for this book is available from the British Library.

ISBN 978-1-912956-36-4

CONTENTS

CONTENTS Cont.

Silent, But Deadly

aplomb	malign	scenic
ascetic	mnemonic	schwa
champagne	nascent	scimitar
consignment	overwrought	sepulchre
ensign	phlegm	succumb
exhortation	psychedelic	synchronous
indictment	rapport	thumbscrew
jostle	rescind	whir
kitsch	resuscitate	wrangle
knickknack	ricochet	writhed

Aaargh!!

acrophobia	hydrophobia	pyrophobia
aerophobia	hypnophobia	technophobia
agoraphobia	necrophobia	toxiphobia
ailurophobia	neophobia	xenophobia
arachnophobia	ophidiophobia	zoophobia
aviophobia	osmophobia	
chemophobia	panophobia	
claustrophobia	pathophobia	
cynophobia	phonophobia	
germophobia	photophobia	

Luck Of The Draw

chance	providential	hapless
coincidental	serendipitous	ill-fated
destined	timely	ill-starred
fluky	unforeseen	infelicitous
fortuitous	unlooked-for	jinxed
fortunate	accursed	luckless
heaven-sent	adverse	ominous
karmic	calamitous	star-crossed
opportune	catastrophic	unfavorable
propitious	doomed	unfortunate

Happy Endings I

apprenticeship	hardship	readership
assistantship	internship	scholarship
authorship	kinship	showmanship
bipartisanship	leadership	statesmanship
censorship	membership	workmanship
championship	ownership	
courtship	partnership	
dictatorship	penmanship	
fellowship	premiership	
friendship	professorship	

The Play's The Thing

act	cues	monologue
apron	curtain call	offstage
aside	dialogue	playwright
audition	downstage	proscenium arch
backstage	dramatis personae	scene
box office	dramaturgy	scenery
callback	dress rehearsal	soliloquy
cast	footlights	thespian
company	interval	understudy
costumes	matinee	upstage

Breaking The Law

abductor	gunrunner	swindler
abettor	hacker	terrorist
arsonist	hijacker	trafficker
assassin	kidnapper	trespasser
burglar	mugger	vandal
cat burglar	murderer	
con artist	pickpocket	
cybercriminal	poacher	
embezzler	smuggler	
gangster	stalker	

Justice Is Served

accusation	hearsay	prosecutor
advocate	imprisonment	punishment
arbitrator	incarceration	rehabilitation
bailiff	innocence	sentence
conviction	jury	verdict
defendant	justice	
deterrent	litigator	
dock	magistrate	
expert witness	offense	
guilt	penalty	

As Dull As Dishwater

banal	lifeless	tedious
bland	mind-numbing	undramatic
boring	monotonous	uneventful
drab	pedestrian	unexciting
dreary	ponderous	unimaginative
dry	prosaic	uninspiring
dull	stale	uninteresting
humdrum	stodgy	unsensational
insipid	stuffy	unspectacular
leaden	suspenseless	vapid

Earth-Shattering

aftershock
amplitude
avalanche
bedrock
cataclysm
conduit
crust
earthshock
epicenter
fault

formations
geology
geophysics
hertz
injurious
intensification
landslide
magnitude
mantle
recurrence

Richter scale
rubble
seismic
seismograph
seismology
shock wave
tectonic
tremor
upheaval
volcanology

Be- The Benighted

becalm
bedeck
befit
befriend
beguile
behead
belabor
belie
belittle
bemire

bemoan
bemuse
beseem
besiege
besmirch
bespeak
bestride
betide
betoken
betroth

bewail
bewitch
befitting
befuddled
bejeweled
benighted
beribboned
besotted
bespoke
bewigged

Make A Splash

alluring	defiantly	nightmarish
Armageddon	deliriously	perilous
audacious	doom	plunged
beauteous	effortlessly	reckoning
bloodbath	engrossment	riveting
breathtaking	enticingly	shattering
celebratory	flawless	tantalize
charismatic	hypnotic	thwarted
colossal	insidious	unabashed
compelled	lurking	vanquish

Gee Whiz...

aggrandize	doggerel	sniggered
aggravation	haggard	staggering
aggregate	juggernaut	suggestive
aggression	laggard	swaggered
aggrieved	loggerhead	thuggee
arpeggios	nugget	thuggery
bedraggled	pettifogger	toboggan
braggadocio	piggyback	toggle
braggarts	priggishness	trigger
doggedly	sluggard	ziggurat

Stop The Presses!

blackout
byline
column
copy editor
copywriter
distribution
editor
editorial
fact-checking
font

fourth estate
gag order
headline
layout
misquotation
objectivity
paragraphing
photojournalist
proofreading
quotations

recanting
redaction
reportage
retraction
shorthand
subscribers
substantiate
tabloid
typesetting
typography

It's Gone Viral

algorithm
analytics
archiving
avatar
bitmoji
block
boosted post
caption
clickbait
crowdsourcing

dashboard
direct message
emoji
engagement
favorite
feed
filter
followers
geotag
handle

hashtag
impressions
influencer
livestream
mention
metric
notification
platform
repost
thread

S Is For Surprised

agape	flabbergasted	stunned
amazed	floored	stupefied
astonished	flummoxed	taken aback
astounded	goggle-eyed	thunderstruck
awestruck	jolted	wide-eyed
benumbed	shell-shocked	
confounded	shocked	
dazed	speechless	
dumbfounded	staggered	
dumbstruck	startled	

Applaud, Or Admonish?

acclaim	laud	chide
adulate	praise	condemn
applaud	revere	criticize
celebrate	salute	lecture
commend	venerate	rebuke
compliment	admonish	reprehend
congratulate	berate	reprimand
extol	castigate	reproach
hail	censure	scold
honor	chastise	upbraid

A Fly In The Ointment

barrier	hindrance	restriction
brick wall	hitch	setback
complication	holdup	snag
constraint	hurdle	stonewall
curb	impediment	stoppage
deterrence	limitation	
drawback	mishap	
embargo	obstacle	
encumbrance	obstruction	
handicap	restraint	

Making Things Easier

accelerating	furtherance	promotion
advancement	galvanization	spur
assistance	goad	stimulant
backing	impetus	stimulation
easing	incentive	stimulus
enabling	inducement	
encouragement	instigation	
expedition	invitation	
facilitation	momentum	
fostering	motivation	

The Roots Of The Matter I

hyperacidity
hyperactive
hyperbola
hyperbolic
hypercritical
hyperinflation
hyperkinetic
hyperlink
hypersensitive
hypersonic

hypertensive
hypertext
hyperthermia
hyperventilate
hypoallergenic
hypochondria
hypocrisy
hypocritical
hypodermic
hypoglycemic

hypomania
hyponym
hypostasis
hypotaxis
hypotensive
hypotenuse
hypothermia
hypothesize
hypothetical
hypoxic

WWI

Allies
armistice
artillery
assassination
casualties
conscription
contraband
convoy
counterattack
doughboy

draft
dreadnought
entente cordiale
front
gas mask
Great War
home front
infantry
land mine
League of Nations

machine gun
mobilization
munition
nationalism
no-man's-land
pacifist
propaganda
treaty
trench warfare
U-boat

Ancient History?

American Dream	lineage	Enlightenment
archivist	memorabilia	Gilded Age
digitization	predecessor	golden age
documentation	regnal year	postbellum
dynastic	repository	Reconstruction
genealogy	Jeffersonian	colonialism
heritage	Lincolniana	imperialism
historiographer	Washingtoniana	industrialization
historiography	antebellum	modernism
Library of Congress	belle epoque	postmodernism

Happy Endings II

auctioneer	muleteer	rocketeer
balladeer	munitioneer	scrutineer
basketeer	musketeer	sloganeer
buccaneer	mutineer	sonneteer
charioteer	orienteer	volunteer
electioneer	pamphleteer	
engineer	privateer	
gazetteer	profiteer	
marketeer	puppeteer	
mountaineer	racketeer	

Win Some, Lose Some

advantageous	remunerative	dissipated
booming	rewarding	failed
enriching	successful	forfeited
flourishing	thriving	gambled
fruitful	worthwhile	impoverished
gainful	deficient	indebted
lucrative	depleted	penalized
productive	deprived	ruined
profitable	destitute	squandered
prosperous	dispossessed	unprofitable

Head-Scratchers

auger	councillor	hoard
augur	counselor	horde
baize	discreet	laps
bays	discrete	lapse
borne	ewe	mean
bourne	yew	mien
censer	faun	throes
censor	fawn	throws
cite	gild	vale
site	guild	veil

TWOFER

advertorial
billboard
blurb
boost
branding
brochure
campaign
circular
commercials
discounting

endorsement
flyer
FOMO
handout
infomercial
jingle
launch
logo
placard
promotional

publicist
publicity
sandwich board
slogan
telemarketing

Brick-&-Mortar

balloon frame
braced frame
brickwork
construction
demolition
development
double glazing
edifice
fabricating
fascia

fenestration
foundation
infrastructure
installation
insulation
jerry-built
maintenance
masonry
partition
planking

planning board
reconstruction
refurbishment
renovation
restoration
roofing
scaffolding
shingle
substructure
superstructure

Mixing Up

absorb	compound	intermingle
amalgamate	conflate	intermix
assimilate	congregate	marry
blend	conjoin	meld
cement	converge	merge
coalesce	fuse	mingle
cohere	homogenize	pool
combine	incorporate	synthesize
commingle	integrate	unify
composite	interfuse	yoke

Before...

ancestor	herald	prefigure
antecedent	overture	prefix
antedate	pioneer	preliminary
anticipate	preamble	prelude
beforehand	precede	premature
curtain-raiser	precedent	premonition
foregoing	precursor	presentiment
forerunner	predate	previous
foreshadow	preexisting	prior
foretaste	preface	prologue

...And After

afterward	ensuing	postscript
belated	epilogue	progeny
closing	eventual	rearmost
concluding	hindmost	resultant
consequent	hindsight	subsequent
crowning	latter	succeeding
deferment	posterity	successive
deferral	posthumous	successor
descendant	postmortem	terminating
endmost	postponement	ultimate

Que-ing Up

appliqué	discotheque	physique
arabesque	goblinesque	picaresque
baroque	grotesque	picturesque
barque	macaque	pique
bisque	marque	plaque
boutique	masque	risqué
burlesque	mosque	statuesque
calque	mystique	technique
communiqué	oblique	torque
critique	opaque	unique

Figuratively Speaking...

allegory	dramatic irony	oxymoron
alliteration	euphemism	paradox
allusion	figure of speech	pathetic fallacy
anaphora	hyperbole	pathos
antithesis	hysteron proteron	personification
apostrophe	irony	pun
assonance	metaphor	sibilance
bathos	metonymy	simile
chiasmus	motif	symbol
contrast	onomatopoeia	synecdoche

Oodles Of Ologies

angelology	ecology	musicology
anthropology	Egyptology	oceanology
bacteriology	epidemiology	oncology
biotechnology	etymology	ophthalmology
cardiology	graphology	ornithology
cosmology	histology	paleontology
criminology	hydrology	pharmacology
cryptology	meteorology	philology
demonology	microbiology	theology
dermatology	mineralogy	toxicology

Eureka!

abstraction
brain wave
brainchild
brainstorm
cognition
concept
conception
conclusion
conjecture
conviction

deduction
formulation
guess
hunch
hypothesis
impression
inspiration
notion
observation
perception

preconception
reflection
speculation
supposition
theory

VEGGING OUT...OR NOT?

apathetic
indolent
inert
lackadaisical
languid
languorous
lethargic
loafing
phlegmatic
shiftless

slothful
sluggardly
sluggish
torpid
work-shy
active
animated
assiduous
conscientious
diligent

dynamic
energetic
indefatigable
industrious
inventive
operative
painstaking
persevering
persistent
tireless

Newton's Cradle

alternating current	conductor	frequency
ampere	convection	half-life
antimatter	decibel	joule
atom	density	newton
calorie	diffraction	particle
cathode ray	diffusion	proton
center of gravity	diode	refraction
centrifugal force	direct current	resistance
centripetal force	electron	spectrum
charge	fission	velocity

Em- Is To Empower

emaciate	embezzle	empathize
emanate	embitter	empeople
emancipate	emblaze	empower
emasculate	emblazon	empurple
embalm	embody	emulsify
embank	embolden	
embark	emboss	
embattle	embower	
embed	embroil	
embellish	empanel	

DOUBLE TROUBLE

allocation
embellishment
hallucination
intelligentsia
malleable
asymmetrical
commercialize
commiserate
consummate
mammalian

apportion
inopportune
puppetry
supplicant
zeppelin
aberration
catarrh
corrugated
extracurricular
surreptitiously

assassinate
connoisseur
disseminate
percussionist
quintessential
attenuate
bloodletting
gluttonous
guttural
intermittency

Happy Endings III

adventuresome
bothersome
burdensome
cuddlesome
cumbersome
fearsome
flavorsome
frolicsome
gamesome
gladsome

gruesome
irksome
lithesome
loathsome
meddlesome
quarrelsome
tiresome
toothsome
twosome
unwholesome

venturesome
wearisome
wholesome
winsome
worrisome

Claim To Fame

acclaimed	prominent	disreputable
celebrated	remarkable	ignominious
distinguished	renowned	iniquitous
eminent	reputable	louche
esteemed	respected	nefarious
exalted	contemptible	notorious
illustrious	delinquent	opprobrious
leading	discreditable	scandalous
legendary	disgraceful	shady
preeminent	dishonorable	troublesome

Wise As An Owl

acuity	insight	sageness
acumen	judgment	sapience
acuteness	judiciousness	savviness
astuteness	keenness	sharpness
canniness	perceptiveness	shrewdness
circumspection	percipience	
clear-sightedness	perspicacity	
cleverness	prudence	
discernment	sagaciousness	
enlightenment	sagacity	

Total Bedlam

anarchy	furor	rampage
bedlam	havoc	riot
chaos	jumble	shambles
commotion	maelstrom	tumult
confusion	mayhem	turbulence
crisis	misorder	turmoil
disarray	misrule	unrest
disorder	muddle	uproar
disorderliness	pandemonium	vortex
fiasco	panic	whirl

Going Without

aridity	famish	scantiness
barrenness	insufficiency	scarcity
blight	lack	severity
dearth	meagerness	shortage
deficiency	paucity	sparsity
deficit	pestilence	starvation
deprivation	poverty	straits
destitution	predicament	suffering
drought	privation	undersupply
emergency	ravagement	want

Short & Sweet

abbreviated	curtailed	shortened
abridged	economical	succinct
aphoristic	encapsulated	summarized
apposite	essential	telegraphic
compact	incisive	truncated
compendious	laconic	
compressed	monosyllabic	
concise	pertinent	
condensed	pithy	
contracted	relevant	

Long-winded

circuitous	interminable	substantial
circumlocutory	lengthy	tortuous
diffuse	loquacious	verbose
digressive	meandering	voluble
discursive	profuse	wordy
embellished	prolix	
embroidered	protracted	
expansive	rambling	
garrulous	repetitious	
inflated	roundabout	

WUNDERBAR!

angst	gesundheit	putsch
bagel	haversack	rucksack
Bauhaus	hinterland	schadenfreude
bildungsroman	kaput	spiel
blitzkrieg	leitmotif	spritz
cobalt	muesli	über-
dachshund	Neanderthal	waltz
delicatessen	poltergeist	wanderlust
doppelgänger	prattle	wunderkind
eiderdown	pretzel	zeitgeist

That Said...

above all	in practice	namely
admittedly	in retrospect	notably
all told	in short	notwithstanding
by the same token	in sum	on balance
completely	in the first place	on the whole
contrastingly	in theory	overall
conversely	inasmuch as	regardless
hence	insofar as	undoubtedly
in all	lest	whereas
in contrast	likewise	wholly

The Roots Of The Matter II

interactive

interdepartmental

interfacial

intergalactic

interlaced

interlinear

interlingual

interlining

interlocking

intermedial

intermediary

interpersonal

intertextual

interwoven

intra-abdominal

intracellular

intracranial

intradermal

intramolecular

intramural

intramuscular

intravenous

introduction

introspective

introverted

Munificent, Or Miserly?

altruistic

ample

bountiful

charitable

copious

cornucopian

fulsome

lavish

liberal

magnanimous

munificent

openhanded

philanthropic

unsparing

unstinting

begrudging

closefisted

frugal

meager

miserly

parsimonious

penny-pinching

penurious

pinchpenny

prudent

scanty

spartan

stingy

stinting

tightfisted

HUE & CRY!

babel	dissent	remonstrance
ballyhoo	eruption	ruckus
brouhaha	ferment	rumpus
cacophony	fracas	unquietness
clamor	hubbub	vociferation
clangor	hullabaloo	
cri de coeur	outburst	
demurral	outcry	
denunciation	protestation	
disputation	racket	

T Is For Trickery

artifice	duplicity	obliquity
betrayal	evasion	oiliness
chicanery	falsehood	shiftiness
covertness	fraudulence	skulduggery
cozenage	furtiveness	slipperiness
cunning	guile	smoke screen
deception	guilefulness	stratagem
dissembling	intrigue	subterfuge
dissimulation	machination	swindling
double-dealing	mendacity	treachery

That Doesn't Look Right...

allegiance	harass	perseverance
atheist	humorous	personnel
camouflage	idiosyncrasy	Portuguese
Caribbean	indict	pronunciation
chauffeur	inoculate	quarantine
colleague	kernel	reference
concede	millennium	supersede
dilemma	omission	upholstery
exhilarate	outrageous	welfare
gauge	pavilion	withhold

OVERT VS. COVERT

aboveboard	plainspoken	enigmatic
acknowledged	straightforward	furtive
avowed	undisguised	implicit
candid	unguarded	secluded
evident	unreserved	secreted
forthright	camouflaged	sneaky
frank	clandestine	subterranean
obvious	classified	surreptitious
outspoken	confidential	unadvertised
overt	covert	underhand

James Bond & Co.

cipher	encryption	reconnaissance
concealment	espionage	recruitment
conspiracies	forgery	sabotage
counterespionage	handler	safe house
counterfeiting	infiltration	secret service
counterintelligence	insider	shadowing
cryptography	intelligence	stealth
decrypting	interception	subversion
disguisement	interrogation	undercover
dupery	mole	underground

Politically Correct?

absolutism	declaration	oppression
abdication	decree	potentate
accession	despotism	revolution
annexation	domination	secession
autocrat	exile	succession
banishment	invasion	supremacy
claimant	monocracy	totalitarianism
coercion	monocrat	unanimity
conspiracy	occupation	unification
cult	oligarchy	usurpation

From Rags To Riches

bankrupt	needful	flush
beggared	needy	loaded
bereft	pauperized	moneyed
broke	penniless	privileged
cash-strapped	poverty-stricken	propertied
distressed	straitened	prospering
impecunious	threadbare	well-fixed
indigent	underprivileged	well-heeled
insolvent	advantaged	well-off
necessitous	affluent	well-to-do

We're Banking On It

account	currency	mortgage
asset	debit	offshore
ATM	deposit	overdraft
bank statement	equity	passbook
banking	Federal Reserve	paycheck
budget	foreign exchange	revenue
capital	income	savings account
cashier	interest	teller
checking account	investment	transaction
credit	liability	withdrawal

A Is For Abecedarian

abecedarian
antiquarian
apiarian
Aquarian
authoritarian
barbarian
disciplinarian
egalitarian
equalitarian
grammarian

hereditarian
humanitarian
libertarian
librarian
millenarian
parliamentarian
pescatarian
predestinarian
proletarian
sectarian

seminarian
totalitarian
utilitarian
vegetarian
veterinarian

HAPPY ENDINGS IV

agelessness
aimlessness
artlessness
bottomlessness
boundlessness
breathlessness
carelessness
cluelessness
effortlessness
endlessness

facelessness
faithlessness
faultlessness
fearlessness
flawlessness
guiltlessness
harmlessness
heartlessness
homelessness
lawlessness

mercilessness
pitilessness
mindlessness
recklessness
relentlessness
remorselessness
ruthlessness
selflessness
thoughtlessness
weightlessness

Out Of Sight, Out Of Mind?

awareness	reminiscence	oblivion
cognizance	retrospection	obliviousness
contemplation	absentmindedness	overlooking
memorials	amnesia	repression
memory	forgetfulness	unawareness
mindfulness	inattention	
nostalgia	inattentiveness	
recall	incognizance	
recollection	nescience	
remembrance	obliteration	

Say Cheese!

aperture	flashbulb	photogenic
camera obscura	focal length	photosensitive
camera script	foreground	pinhole camera
capture	frame	projection
close-up	ghosting	red-eye
contact print	grain	resolution
darkroom	negative	selfie
digital camera	overexposure	sepia
exposure	photo shoot	snapshot
flash	photobombing	zoom lens

C-eeing Double

accede	eccentricity	occult
accelerant	ecclesiastical	occupancy
accentuate	fettuccine	saccharine
accessory	Fibonacci	staccato
accidental	flaccid	stuccowork
acclimatize	impeccably	succinctly
accolade	inaccuracies	succor
baccalaureate	occasioned	succulent
bacchanalian	Occident	succumbing
desiccated	occlude	vaccinate

I Don't Feel So Good

anorexia	gout	polio
appendicitis	hepatitis	rabies
arthritis	hypertension	rheumatism
bronchitis	influenza	salmonella
bulimia	leprosy	sciatica
chicken pox	malaria	shingles
cholera	measles	tuberculosis
common cold	meningitis	typhoid fever
diabetes	mumps	whooping cough
dysentery	pneumonia	yellow fever

A Rapid Rise...

accelerate	escalate	promote
accumulate	exacerbate	redouble
amplify	expand	skyrocket
appreciate	extend	snowball
ascend	heighten	soar
aspire	intensify	surge
augment	mount	uplift
burgeon	multiply	uprear
dilate	mushroom	upturn
elevate	proliferate	wax

...OR A SLOW DECLINE?

abate	demote	plummet
collapse	deplete	plunge
compress	depreciate	recede
contract	deteriorate	reduce
debase	devolve	relax
decimate	diminish	shrink
decline	downscale	slump
de-escalate	downsize	subside
deflate	dwindle	tumble
degenerate	ebb	wane

The Roots Of The Matter III

benediction
benedictory
benefactor
benefactress
beneficence
beneficial
beneficiary
benefit
benevolence
benign

benison
maladapted
maladjusted
maladministration
malady
malaise
malcontent
malediction
malefactor
malfeasance

malformed
malice
malignant
malnutrition
malodorous

Happy Endings V

analgesic
antagonistic
chimeric
didactic
eclectic
elliptic
empathetic
erratic
hydraulic
idiosyncratic

impressionistic
kinetic
neurotic
opportunistic
peripatetic
philharmonic
pluralistic
problematic
quadraphonic
quixotic

rhapsodic
ritualistic
sardonic
soporific
sporadic
stoic
symptomatic
systemic
talismanic
therapeutic

Above Or Below Par?

adept
authority
expert
fiend
maestro
master
professional
proficient
pundit
savant

scholar
specialist
virtuoso
whiz
wizard
amateur
apprentice
dabbler
dilettante
fledgling

freshman
hobbyist
inexpert
initiate
jack-of-all-trades
layperson
neophyte
nonprofessional
novice
tyro

Body Language

abdomen
aorta
appendix
arteries
bone marrow
bronchi
capillaries
cartilage
cerebrum
circulation

cranium
diaphragm
esophagus
gallbladder
larynx
ligaments
lymph nodes
pancreas
pharynx
sinews

spinal cord
spleen
tendon
thyroid
tonsils
torso
trachea
veins
ventricle
vertebrae

HOW DO YOU SAY THAT?!

adolescence
aegis
annals
awry
brooch
cache
crinoline
dishabille
espresso
flautist

foyer
glower
gyro
macabre
mascarpone
mauve
meme
meringue
moniker
niche

peremptory
regime
rendezvous
sergeant
sherbet
sorbet
statistics
wrath
wreath
wyvern

THAT'S A PROPER WORD?!

blatherskite
bloviation
bombastic
bunkum
caboodle
cacography
fatuous
fisticuffs
flibbertigibbet
flimflam

gallimaufry
gewgaw
hodgepodge
kerfuffle
killjoy
kowtow
lugubrious
mishmash
murmuration
namby-pamby

nincompoop
persnickety
quicksilver
razzle-dazzle
razzmatazz
shebang
shenanigans
switcheroo
tidbit
whirligig

INDEX

In the following entries, the letter 'A' refers to the upper list on the page, while 'B' refers to the lower one.